The Awe and The Awful

poems by

Charles Lattimore Howard

2013

A portion of the proceeds from the sale of *The Awe and The Awful* will be donated to those who work to stem the tide of gun violence and support institutions that serve individuals experiencing homelessness.

Published by Bernstein Liebe
Cherry Hill, NJ 08034
www.BernsteinLiebe.com
We are proud of this publication; please forward your comments to info@bernsteinliebe.com.

Cover design by NickRichGFX.com

Produced in the United States of America
10 9 8 7 6 5 4 3 2
ISBN 13: 978-1-4827-6384-3
ISBN 10: 1-4827-6384-2

I am in awe when I look into the eyes of my beloved wife.

Thank you, Lia, for being my best friend and my love.
It is to you and our girls,
who have taught me much about art, creativity and imagination,
that I dedicate this project.

Soli Deo gloria.

Contents

The Awe and The Awful

Part I

We are the awe and the awful.
Fearfully and wonderfully made.
We
Full of dreams
And imagination
With enough love to pray for a world without hunger, or poverty, or war.
And enough faith to hold on and keep loving
Until we get there.

But awful, too.
Too much killing
Awfully selfish
Awfully fearful
Not wonderful.
"Humans are complex,"
they told me.
"We're all in process,"
they said.

We are the awe and the awful.
And me, too.

I see in mirrors
Soul in color
Life in death
Hope for orphans.

And I see myself
Drowning in insecurities
Pride
Stupid pride.
Over self-medicating.

In mirrors I see the —
How did Maya phrase it? —
"The hope of the slave"
But still in chains.
Born free
Running back and forth
From North to South
From Plantation to River
Plantation to River.

We are the awful.
But the awed is with us
And in us.

We are, to a lesser extent, the awed.
But the awful is all around us.
And
forgive
in us as well.

The seraphim uncover their eyes and look with awe
Especially when we approach the awful.
With pity when we don't.
Humans.

The Awe and The Awful

Part 2

In holy moments
In thin places
Butterflies land on me.
I am filled with awe
At beauty
At trust
At a moment so sacred I dare not breathe or move.

I feel special
Blessed.
So blessed.
Remembered.
And reminded that new life is possible.

That maybe God sees who we could be
And not just who we have been.

That our Creator sees us flying.

That awful is not the end.

We are the awe and the awful
Like caterpillar butterflies
Like tears – weeping and rejoicing from the same eyes.

We are the awe and the awful
I pray we can see both
See it all.
That we can fly to flowers that inspire awe.

But that we also land on the awful —
Even for a holy moment in a thin place.
Thin places are where the awe and the awful meet.
Maybe the wind will take us there.
And carry us away.

Orphans and Widows

Orphans and widows pray differently
seldom with words.
We pray with light
and water
breezes and gusts.

Some widows and widowers pray with bottles.
Wine for our spirits.

Most orphans pray with their feet
not like Heschel
not for protest
but for protection.
Never getting too close to those
who might love and leave.

Our prayers are always laced with tears
And never in the dark.
I pray best indoors — alone
with a window open because you never know who might come in.

We don't pray that they'll come back.
Wouldn't do that to them.
And I only rarely pray to go to them
Though I'm ready.

When we pray
We just sit there.
My heart and eyes do all the talking necessary.
Resting in invisible but
Absolutely felt arms.

Known Depths

Part I

Some poems take a lifetime to write
resting in the shade of broken hearts
untouched by the healing light of the sun.
Maybe that's what poetry is,
diving into darkness
bringing words to light.
Some words tied to some memories
have lived for decades in a
grey stillness.
An angel with a flaming sword
guards the gate to this shaded place.
I return now
to wrestle with the angel
to go back in
to not only bring words to light,
but to bring light to memories
from long ago.

I am afraid, like that little boy that I see still sitting in the shade
trembling after holding his dying mother in his arms.
I am undone, like the teenager at his father's side
walking with him to death's door.
He's quiet
sitting in the shade, too.

I don't want to see them
but the first words they say to me are
"It's time."

It's taken a lifetime for me to go back in.
Maybe light will follow me and heal a broken heart.

Known Depths

Part 2

After your second parent dies
you begin to think that you are cursed
that anyone whom you get close to
anyone whom you love
you will also lose.

Thus, you love in the only way your heart can bear
very slowly
yet afraid.
If your loved one is just a few minutes late
you fear the worst
and begin to imagine afterlife
having already lived two.

Loving hurts too much
so you patch up the cracks in your heart with quick intimacy.
No love involved
a lot of like
but inevitably it comes
Love.
You can't help but love,
hoping he or she will fill in for the lost.

That's it. The cursed love on an orphan.
You either fear love
so you get real close real quick

and then cut and run
or you make quick mother figures and father figures
of others who can't possibly stay.
Damned orphan love.

Known Depths

Part 3

Maybe someday I will be able to receive love again.
I suppose in my case, it's been the worst and the best
thing that has ever happened to me.
A curse and a blessing.
I would not be who I am
able to feel, see, and hear pain

to know depths is to have lived
to draw from them is to have loved

Orphans
I believe
either run away from God in fear and resentment
or love him harder.
He, their only parent
can't die on them
won't leave them on a stranger's steps.

I've known depths
But I've been pulled out and
loved.

a prayer before preaching

how shall we approach You...
Love Itself,
Whose majesty is beyond description
Whose glory is beyond what our eyes can bear
Whose likeness is beyond any words our lips can articulate.
why do we not tremble when we consider just Who it is we are
addressing?
how shall we approach you?
with what feeble, unworthy, words?

perhaps our Quaker brothers and sisters have it right.
better to sit in expectant silence
than to ramble on with
words without knowledge.
and so as i mount this pulpit
and dare to approach the One true Word,
with inadequate sentences —
i ask Your forgiveness.
Amen.

Missing the Question, Missing the Mark

Might sin not always be what it seems?
I sinned once... (I say with a smile)
and the guilt was nearly unbearable. (I say with a frown)
Somewhere between the self-hatred
and the fear of punishment (all sentences I absolve you of)
I stumbled on a question.

Might there be more to sin than just "bad"
than just "missing the mark?"
I thought, without going so far as to say He willed it or is delighted that
I've done it,
"Might He be using this for some purpose?"
Humility?
Reliance on Him?
Compassion for others?
Low wisdom?

We are forgiven.
And there's more.

Grace

Grace is far more than pardon from sin.
That is the easiest part, perhaps the least important part.
Grace is, rather, the fact that we are known, fully known, by God
and yet still loved.
Grace is the fact that God understands us
and understands what is behind our sins.

A sweet friend named Annemarie once told me that
"Fear is the garden of sin."

God, in God's sovereignty,
knows the painful childhood experiences,
the insecurities,
the unhealed hurts,
the shattered dreams,
indeed the garden,
from which our sin emerges.

This does not mean that we get a pass or that it's okay to sin simply
because God understands.
No
we must ever strive to heal
(or rather receive God's healing in our lives).

What it does mean is that we are fully known and fully loved.
Might we, when we are the victim of sin or witness others missing the
mark,
be able to see them with holy eyes?
Eyes that can see past the act into the dirt and soil where its roots lie
hidden?
And then what?

Come in!

When the soul is at last brought before the judgment seat of Love,
the question asked will not be
"How many rules did she break?"
Nor will one hear
"How was his theology?'
It will not be asked
"Was she on the right side of the most contentious issues of her day?"

The questions asked will be

"Did he love?"

and

"Was he loved?"

And a voice will cry out from One whose face shines like the sun
With joy in His tone, He will say,
"Yes! I loved Him!
Come in! Come in! My beloved, come in!"

"I believe!"

It was not until several years into his ministry that brother Wesley at last converted.
One can almost audibly hear over these centuries his words — "I believe!"
What got him was this notion of
love without requirement — save our reception of that love —
if even that.
It is not our holiness that saves us,
but praise God, it is the Lord who saves by, with, and in love.
Likewise, is it the same with not just salvation, but sanctification as well?
Is it God who sanctifies rather than us making ourselves holy?
Is it God who makes a great preacher great, a masterful professor effectual?

I want to love like this.
Loving without requirement.
Without a need of compensation
Without the need for the beloved
to be kind
or nice
or appreciative.
God loves us
even when our works and life do not deserve it.

Oh, the joyful surprise the sinner must feel the moment after death,
when arms of grace
catch them on the other side!
When knowing that this life only deserves Hell,
He is there offering love one more time,
even after a life of selfishness and fear.
He offers life!
Oh, happy day for the sad!

How can this love be!?
So much more than any human can love!
Lord, give me a portion of this love —
this amazing love!
It has little to do with us,
this does not pivot on my behavior but...on His Love.

What of the poor? I am the poor!
My God, I so joyfully come to your door, your table, begging with open hands.
And you never turn me away — no matter how needy I am.
You give knowing I will sin again
(Unlike me, who seldom trusts after I so hesitantly give,
demanding the beggar doesn't buy drink with the dollar I barely shared with him.)
I came homeless and orphaned to your door
and You opened it up,
brought me in. Adoption!
You adopted me and changed my name.
My Father, you saved me!
May I never turn one away. Not one, I pray.

Ambition

Do not strive to be great,
But rather strive to do great things for God.
Why is humility so important to You?
You do not desire us to be great or perfect.
You do not require or expect us to be without sin.
You challenge us to be humble –
not seeking a glory that belongs to you alone.
Not seeking recognition.
Could I write books without my name on them?
Could I bless others without being thanked or without them knowing?
Do not strive to be great,
But rather strive to do great things for God.
Rather than having hopes to become the next
Mother Teresa, Ghandi or Martin King,
might we simply have hope and work to end
poverty –
even if our names are never etched into the bases of sculptures.
Do not strive to be great,
But rather strive to do great things.

The Road to Sainthood

How does one become a saint?
Is it a result of effort and determination?
Is it a gift of grace?
Do we work to become saints
or are we made into saints?
What lies within our desire for sainthood?
Is it a pious pride desiring canonization,
recognition of our holiness?
Or is it desire to make The Saint-maker proud and beam a divine
smile.

Maybe the journey to sainthood begins "simply"
with an act of receiving
love and loving
without care of ever being called
saint.

Truth

No one's got it all.
Neither side, neither nation,
neither denomination –
neither of us.
For who can capture the truth?
Truth – absolute truth (also known as love) does indeed exist,
but who can possess or wrap one's arms around something bigger than
one's self?

Ashes

Where are the stairs that lead up to the sky?
Something in the blur is calling to me.
I am out of breath even before one step.

God, You take my breath away.

"Then, my love, you have already climbed the first step,
For awe at the vastness, ungraspable Blue is the beginning of the climb.
You have taken another step when you are willing to dismount the stairs,
abandoning the desire to climb.
Then replace it with a desire for the One who waits above."

Panting, I lay upon the ground,
anxious to see You,
breathing heavy after running in stillness.
Dying but never dead.
Dying to self and living in Love.
I've found the stairs and fallen from them.
Fallen and then saved… and carried up.

Dancing Love

Do You sing to me as I sing to You?
Do You long for me like I long for You?
Do You desire to come to me
like my heart nearly escapes this chest,
desiring to fly to You?

But how can One who needs nothing want me?

My love, You invite me to dance, to leave, to live.
When will You take me? I will not hesitate.
You call me into the music — to get lost in Your song.
We dance like there are no others on the dance floor.
My God, don't let this song end.
You whisper to me, my answer is and always will be "yes."
I hang onto this moment desperately... please, please don't let this song
end.

I hold you too tightly
(*Never too tight, You say*).
You whisper to me secrets no word is worthy to robe.
My answer is and will always be "yes" —
Call me to a new place, set me apart.
You, who need nothing, yet want me.
You want me, You want me, My God, You want me.

Down Here My Love

Is it wrong to want You,
to desire You.
To feel something within me,
something reaching out for You.
To hold,
to possess the unpossessible?

I need You right here.
Please come to me, my Love -
Call me when You get this...

Till then, I will wait with watchful eyes
at my window,
longing for Your return.

A reply!
Ahhh – a letter slid under my door.
From You! You've reached out to me!

Meet me in the streets of the city.
I am waiting there for you.

I race out my door,
running into the dark with only the
light of love
showing the way.

Look down, my love.
I am here dressed in rags,
crowned with poverty.
Homeless as I ever was.

I dwell with the beggars.
Am I still your desire?
Here away from the large cathedrals,
from the wealth of your churches,
from the power of your leaders?
Here, at the bottom,
will you come down and love these, my sisters and brothers,
and then love Me?

In Search of Absurdity

When did we lose absurdity?
That which was once absurd,
once described as madness,
is now commonplace.

A man froze to death today —

"I didn't see that in the news..."

Another child shot —

"WHY GUNS?"

When did we lose a sense of the absurd?
When did having neighbors, fellow citizens, fellow humans
sleep on the street,
die of malnutrition and starvation,
stop
being absurd and simply become accepted?

"Not my problem."

Who among us has the courage to be absurd now?
To believe and hope against present realities, present norms?
Who will dare to break away from the common,
to feel instead of being numb,
to wake up instead of being asleep,
to care?
Is even caring absurd now?

Make me crazy for you, Lord.
I pray you wake me up to that which is absurd and abhorrent to you.
And then create in me a courage that is absurd to the world
And I will care as you do, with an absurd love.

Indifference: A Ramble

Me and Dixon were on the late shift.
Homeless outreach.
Got some off of the street
some into detox
some into rehab
some into the psych ward.
Others just needed a bed.

Too many stories,
Many souls.

It's been a long time now.
Just flashes of faces, moments.
I remember the Puerto Rican addicts
who came up to Philly believing they were
signed up for a rehab program
that would provide treatment
jobs
counseling
housing.

They got hustled.
And then they got high.
I have never seen so many drugs in one place.

Me and Dixon found them under a bridge,
Trying to O.D.
They said they were **trying** to O.D.
Nothing lost in translation.

~

Then there were the hard core guys.
Most stay on the street during the hot Philly summers.
Some last through the fall.
Only a few, out of loathing for the shelters
or mental illness
or genius
or for all of those reasons
stay out through the winter.

They prefer the freedom
the autonomy
the reliance upon God, they'd say.
Nobody's stealing from them out here.
That's not true, of course.

Shame that some folks feel safer on the street
than in shelters.

Many Souls.
Bag ladies with everything they own
in bags that are pillows.
Winos
who are trapped in addictions
that chain them to the street.

Did you ever think about how hard it is
to find somewhere to go to the bathroom
when you're homeless?

NO PUBLIC RESTROOMS
RESTROOMS FOR CUSTOMERS ONLY

So they go outside.

$100 fine.
Fine.
Too many fines – jail.
Fine.
Indifference.

Lot of vets out there, too.
Still fighting.

Women –
Usually there because they were running.
They'd rather sleep outside
than be hit again.
As dangerous as the street is,
they think it's safer than being there
with him.

Did you ever notice the benches?
Some of those are beds, ya know?
And the ones the city doesn't want to be beds anymore
they put a bar right in the middle of it.
Not decoration.
Not just an arm rest.
Try sleeping on that.
Indifference.

Ya know when I was living up north,
some kids started to light homeless guys on fire.
Some just punch them and take their anger out on them.
Nobody cares.

The women on the street
Too often raped.

No police report.
Nobody cares.

Me and Dixon did a funeral on a bench once.
A man froze there.
'bout ten people staring at an empty bench while I read ancient words.
Indifference.
Nobody cares.

Matthew Works
opened my eyes.
"Why do churches lock their doors?
Why not open them up for homeless people to sleep there?"

Indifference.

Teach us to care.

~

Involuntarily committing someone is among the worst things one
may ever have to do.
Me and Dixon did it.

"A DANGER TO OTHERS OR THEMSELVES."

Discreetly call the police and the mental health van...
It's as bad as you imagine.
Screaming
NO! NO! GET OFF ME!
I'M NOT CRAZY!
PLEEEEEEEAAAAAASSSSSSE!

Gone.

And then back again 30 days later.

Indifference.

The point isn't really to get them off the street.
It's to get them out of the cycle.
To reintegrate them back into a society that is indifferent.

Me and Dixon tried.
Help me to keep tryin', Lord. To not be
Indifferent.
Involuntarily committed.

We're all crazy.

There are no fish

She prayed everyday that I would become a monk,
but when I was growing up, I wanted to be a fisherman
Just like my father
And my father's father
And the disciples John and James (more like John).

And anyone who wants to fish
for their life (not just for sport)
does so not because they enjoy catching fish.
A hunter who enjoys killing fearful animals is a coward.
These fish are our little sisters and brothers.
I thank them each, one by one, when they come in.

I wanted to fish because of —
Have you ever laid flat in the middle of a boat
under a full moon
while gently being rocked by waves that seem to love you back?
Have you been the only sound
early in the morning under a sun that reveals only a glimpse into God's glory?
I fish because I can pray all day in my floating cell
with swimming brothers and sisters who've made life vows.

I thank them each, one by one, when they come in.
I used to, at least.

Now after long days, I come back sun burned
and tell hungry neighbors,
"There are no fish."

Large boats driven by faces with lighter skin than mine
drag large nets destroying the coral reef
destroying a balance
destroying a vocation
a life.

"There are no fish"
They're all sitting in a freezer in Paris, in London, or Madrid.

Fish can go, but not me.
I'm illegal.
My sisters and brothers, my living
pulled out of the water and thrown on ice.

I don't want to fish anymore. What would my father say?
What would James say?
"Consider it pure joy…"

Drowning

It is dangerous to swim in rivers...
My tears fall in peaceful solitude
Yet You are here.
With my past, my now, my someday
All washed away... but You.
Just water, flowing, cleansing, quenching,
Moving me.
Why do I weep so? Is it the light hitting the water?
(I was born by the water in Baltimore, you know)
Come into me like the light enters the water, so easily, so perfectly.
Pull me under.
I can't breathe —
Oh, to drown in You —
Pull me in like light beneath the space where air and water meet.
Why do I weep so? Because I know I must go back to the banks and leave
this — leave You.
I try to pick You up, and hold You, but You are uncontainable,
uncontrollable, like this river.
Always alive, always present, always here. Always.
I weep because I can't hold You in my arms.

To drown in You. To be pulled under and then to be saved.
That is salvation.

Minister's Lament

Should I take my collar off before I cry?
They told me early
A minister's life is lonely.

It is.

On for everyone,
"bearing everyone's burdens."
I bring their prayers, hopes, hurts
To You
I bring Your hopes, hurts, bread
To them.
Who brings anything to me?
Who will tell me it's going to be alright?

Silence.

No dark nights here.
My soul stands alone at dusk
I will not let go of the day.

Utter emptiness in this room, this confessional
I have no one save You.
My God, you save
Those who have no one.
My tears are lost in a sea of hope.

Remember me.

My sin is different.
My confession is of doubt.

Fear that You won't be there tomorrow.
There I said it.
Doubt.
And rather than enter a darkness where You may not be,
I rest here with orange and pink skies
Where I'm sure.

Yet I cry because I know I'm called into the darkness.
Some places ministers must enter.
Through doubt. Through the night.
Slowly, one tear at a time.
But the good news is —
Morning always comes.

For whom do I cry?

What is this that shakes me
and pulls tears from my searching brown eyes?
What guides me to the street?
What is this that warms my heart and tingles my soul?
For what or for whom do I cry?
Me? The little orphan, sun kissed after long urban desert walks?
Them? Waiting on the margins of an unwritten page?
Tears of love for You? Longing for You? Shame in front of You?
Help me to remember
And not forget.

Names of lost ones from shoulder to wrist worn like a sleeve.
Both arms.
Unnamed parents on there somewhere.
I don't want to forget them.
They walk with me everywhere.
They help me lift
That which is too heavy.

Like You.
I can't wrap my arms around You by myself
But when the names on my arms – my people who are with You already –
Help me, I get closer.

I see.
Tears for the streets.
Because You and my people
Are there.
Never again will I wipe my tears.
At least not until all of these little ones come home.

Come Slowly

Shake my soul.
Thoughts of you
Shake my soul.
Too much love.
Tears, again, tears.

I will keep quiet.
I will not address you with words that will always fall short.
Seal my lips together.
I will not speak again.
Search my heart and know of my love for you.
See my wet face and know of my soul's longing to fly back to you.
My soul shakes, my soul shakes
With sighs, moans, love beyond words.
Free me from this body that I may fly to you,
But I come slowly — one tear at a time.
Again, tears.

Pathway

Rumi believed that the pathway to God
was through poetry, the arts, and dance.
Perhaps I'd replace pathway
with window.
For poetry, the arts, music, and dance tell all truth, as Emily said, but they
"tell it slant."
Not slanted with a distortion or corruption, not slanted with an
intentionally distorted mis-lead,
but rather the truth, in the arts, is told in holy mystery.

The Upanishads refer to God as
"(The One) before whom all words recoil."
Words, in their normal parade of irreverence,
so easily spilled from my lips, fall carelessly on a page trying in vain to
paint a picture or capture
the incapturable.
Yet, when my words are at last undomesticated, set free into the wild of
poetry
or even
Dissolved into oil and painted or planted into my body as the dry seeds
they are,
Living Water brings them
to life and they grow and they grow and they grow
upward toward Heaven, inward taking root, and by grace,
they flower.
I do believe there is only One path Way.
Only One door.
But maybe there are a number of windows through
Which light may come and hit our faces.

Sincerity

The Rebbe spoke of sincerity. To not approach The One with, "Words
without knowledge."
I will not speak then. I know far too little.
And when I dare utter even the smallest of prayers,
I shall do so with reverence, with trembling, with
gratitude and with love. How dare I

Prophetic Preaching

What might prophetic preaching sound like?

Sweetest rage or a burning ardent love?
Righteous loathing over a wounded dove?
Words to open ears, eyes, hearts, hand,
Hope to drown fears, my past demands?

Prophesy, piety, preaching
Held up like a triptych icon

I see futures past

The now in the Way.
Change in our day.
Words we must say.

Prophesy, piety, preaching
Painted like Rublev

Sharing a table
Opened to me
They want me to be
Able to see.

A life full of love –
Reading like rhyme schemes subtly breaking rules
Not to spite,
But for freedom
And not just the preacher's.

Grace, too

What mystery is greater than the why which lies within the mystery of
God?
Two Whys!
Why is it given? And why to me?
Why to me... is it because you know me?
Because you were there when my father beat me...
Because you were there when they told me I couldn't do it...
'Cause you were there when they called me ugly,
called me fat,
called me stupid...
didn't call me.
Is it because you know my loneliness,
You know I've never been the same since she died?
Why?
I would've left me alone a long time ago.
How do you love like this?
And why don't I?
What mystery is greater than Your grace and Your love?
I want to love like this –
With an amazing grace that understands why.
With a grace that need not even understand at all.
I pray for this.
How can I not love as I have been loved?

Just Beyond Words

When shall I meet You, my Love,
my secret admirer — or one I've secretly admired for so long.
Do you beckon me come to the silence?
Shall I fall into humble darkness?
Will You catch me there?
Are You and are You not in tension?
In deepening contradiction?
Irony?
Or do You wait just beyond my words
and inadequate delaying sentences?
Is that You reaching for me on the other side of my fears?
Or are You much closer than that?
Dancing with me making music in my heart.
Oh, let me come to You (dance with You).
Do You wear a mask?
Waiting with patient hope for me to approach You
as You hide behind the eyes of the poor,
in the smile of the orphan
Never Orphaned.

A Few More Days

I come to you.
You come to me, too!
To meet me half way?
Or am I blind and
unaware of what this week holds?
Then I pray You take me into that quiet place just over there.
I will empty my pockets,
unlace my shoes,
pick up my cloak from the dusty ground. No more waving palm branches.
Oh Love, beyond four letters, I will not betray you. Today

Awful Joy

Will You run with me?
Run through cracked fire hydrant streams.
Water hitting our faces – Black, Brown, Yellow, White laughter with
clear water cooling on
100 degree days.

Run through black top courts with orange spheres moving through chain
nets.
Brothas playing harder than the pros.
God knows.

Run through forgotten streets
where they'd be surprised at how much joy really is down here.
Like joy in North Philly,
Joy in East L.A.,
Joy in Southside Chicago,
Joy in North Baltimore,
Joy in Matapan,
Joy in Spanish Harlem.

Will you run with me by boarded up houses where squatters crash,
laughing at old jokes, making sense out of madness?
Through the city shelter, where old friends laugh at careless supervisors
Through black robed courts with orange suited brothas moving with
chained hands.
Brothas trying to make it to another day.
God knows.

Run through forgotten streets
where they'd be surprised at how much joy really is down here.
Like joy in Cape Town,

Joy in Accra,
Joy in Kingston,
Joy in Sao Paolo,
Joy in Port au Prince,
Joy in my heart.

Refugee's Return

Someday you'll come back
and want to know –
"Why didn't you want me?"
And I too will have a question –
"Is child sacrifice always a sin?"
The binding of Isaac
was not wrong in itself.
And I heard no angels telling me to stop!
I gave you up so that you could live
So that you could be loved...

All of your siblings are dead.
You are speaking to unmarked graves.
A village that no longer exists.
All of my children died
before they even knew what genocide was.
Don't speak to me of child sacrifice.
I laid you on the altar... it was my life that was sacrificed!
And I did want you – every day.
Wondering what you looked like
what your new favorite toys were.
If you remembered me – hoping that you didn't
So that you would not feel the hole in your chest that I feel
every time I saw a mother holding a child.
For months, I still felt the birth pains
but no matter how hard I pushed...
You never ended up in my arms.
It was me crying.
Me.
Someday you'll come back and want to know –
"What happened to my people?"

You'll want to know your birth name.
It is not Isaac.
It is written gently on the dust that guards your birthplace.
That tells the wordless story of what happened here.
It is written on the ash of burned homes.
It is resting on my lips
Just over there.

Pray to God. Maybe I'll be invited close enough to listen in.
And then, little one, listen for the reply.
I'll watch my grandchildren while they're at school.
I'll send friends to help you not forget.
And I'll be just over there. Never too far.

Someday. Your name is Someday.

Mid-Weak

Between Palm branches and Pilate
Hosanna and Herod
I'm reminded that I am
human

Miles (Maundy Thursday)

Wash a Homeless man's feet.
Your friend at church —
Too easy.

Get down on your knees on the concrete of the city.
A chair in fellowship hall —
Too easy.

Take water, a towel. And remember
From whom you learned this.

Look closely at his feet.
See the miles.
The body keeps score.

Take water, a mirror. And remember
Who is really being washed.

Mourning Miss Robyn (Good Friday)

My mother cooked cocaine so I could go to school.
Not easy to fill out college applications with the sound of cracking
product in the kitchen.

"Mom, what should I write down for parent's occupation?"

"...Crossing Guard."

You see my mom had two jobs. Fully human and fully divine.
Every morning "Miss Robyn" would wear the orange and black reflective
vest
in the spring
coat in the winter
And make sure her babies got to school safely.
Putting herself in traffic
so they — so we — didn't have to.
All the while, I was too embarrassed to call her mom.

"Morning, Miss Robyn!"

The crazy thing was my mother went to school to learn how to cook —
Not coke. She wanted to be a chef, open a restaurant and cook her way
to a new life.
To resurrection.
Now she's stuck on this cross
This crossing guard day job
And her night job... cooking.
All so that we might have a different life than her.

For freedom.

Unlike my classmates, I didn't have a job in the family business waiting
for me.
I'm not allowed to come back to the nest.

"Spread your wings and fly, baby."

And so I flew as far away from my nest of cracked eggs and
shameful walks from my orange and Black mother
who lived Good Friday every single day —
for me.

I pray that one day I'll come back on Easter and not find her here.
No longer crossing for little kids who don't appreciate the complexity or
depth of her love.
That's real love.

Put that in your pipe and smoke it.

Saturdays (Holy Saturday)

It is a short walk from Friday to Saturday.
This unutterable truth is hidden until it reveals itself to you,
Emerging out of waiting
with suffering and ecstasy written on each hand.
Her left hand has touched me more than I care to write or speak of —
No words, only groans, sobs, tears, fists beating a bursting chest.
And her right lifts my head upwards.
Draws my heart outward.
What can I say —
no words, only moans, smiles, head shakes, and "happy tears" as my
daughter calls them.
This is life.
This is living with both hands.
But what of the rest?
Life between this and that?
Saturday?
Saturday is waiting.
Is it more?
Maybe it is also moving
between suffering and ecstasy
from death to resurrection.
His and ours.

Risen (Easter Morning)

When the sun rises
And gently shines into our rooms
On Easter mornings
We should rise up, too.

Disrobe.
Take off what they buried you in.
They thought you would wear these burial clothes forever.
Your arms, they folded, perhaps crossing them over your chest

Missing the irony of it all.

And then you were
clothed in tear stained garments with little if any hope.

Far off, either miles or millennia away,
a voice sings;

"Were you there when they laid Him in the grave..."

Sometimes.

That's where most of our stories end.
Buried in graves that were not meant for us.
Buried in clothes that others gave us.
But the author of our lives is not done writing yet.

All of us, like the Nazarene, bear crosses.
And all of us at times find ourselves buried and wrapped in what we are
forced to wear.

But it's Easter. For us, too.
The stone trapping us in has been rolled away.
We are free.
We are saved.
We are alive again.
And like the Resurrected One,
We should rise up, too.
Come out of the dark
And walk out the cave.
Greet the Angels on the side and give them their lines.
"When they come to see me, tell them, *I am not here. I am risen.*"

Made in the USA
San Bernardino, CA
22 June 2014